SPORTS

GENDER
AND RACE
IN SPORTS

BY DUCHESS HARRIS, JD, PHD
WITH KATE CONLEY

Essential Library

An Imprint of Abdo Publishing | abdobooks.com

ABDOBOOKS.COM

Published by Abdo Publishing, a division of ABDO, PO Box 398166, Minneapolis, Minnesota 55439. Copyright © 2019 by Abdo Consulting Group, Inc. International copyrights reserved in all countries. No part of this book may be reproduced in any form without written permission from the publisher. Essential Library™ is a trademark and logo of Abdo Publishing.

Printed in the United States of America, North Mankato, Minnesota.
092018
012019

 THIS BOOK CONTAINS
RECYCLED MATERIALS

Cover Photo: Liu Zishan/Shutterstock Images
Interior Photos: AP Images, 5, 8, 15, 22, 75; Bill Chaplis/AP Images, 10; Julian Finney/Getty Images, 12; Katherine Frey/Washington Post/Getty Images, 19; Jorge Lemus/NurPhoto/Sipa/AP Images, 25; Rick Bowmer/AP Images, 28; Oleksandr Berezko/Shutterstock Images, 31; Sergey Novikov/Shutterstock Images, 34; Richard C. Lewis/Icon Sportswire/AP Images, 37; Anucha Maneechote/Shutterstock Images, 39; Vasha Hunt/AL.com/AP Images, 44; Eric Risberg/AP Images, 47; Daniel A. Anderson/Cal Sport Media/AP Images, 51; Kazuki Wakasugi/Yomiuri Shimbun/AP Images, 54; Michael Caulfield/AP Images, 59; David Dennis/Icon Sportswire/AP Images, 62; Quinn Harris/Icon Sportswire/AP Images, 65; Red Line Editorial, 67; Mark J. Terrill/AP Images, 68; Chuck Myers/Cal Sports Media/AP Images, 73; Gregory Bull/AP Images, 79; Mike Derer/AP Images, 82; Eric Christian Smith/AP Images, 85; Paul Morigi/Invision/espnW/AP Images, 87; Ed Ou/AP Images, 89; Darron Cummings/AP Images, 94; Aaron M. Sprecher/CHERA/AP Images, 97; Yawar Nazir/Getty Images, 98

Editor: Patrick Donnelly
Series Designer: Craig Hinton

LIBRARY OF CONGRESS CONTROL NUMBER: 2018947972

PUBLISHER'S CATALOGING-IN-PUBLICATION DATA

Names: Harris, Duchess, author. | Conley, Kate, author.
Title: Gender and race in sports / by Duchess Harris and Kate Conley.
Description: Minneapolis, Minnesota : Abdo Publishing, 2019 | Series: Race and sports | Includes online resources and index.
Identifiers: ISBN 9781532116704 (lib. bdg.) | ISBN 9781641856225 (pbk) | ISBN 9781532159541 (ebook)
Subjects: LCSH: Sex discrimination in sports--Juvenile literature. | Racism in sports--Juvenile literature. | Sports--Juvenile literature. | Race relations--Juvenile literature.
Classification: DDC 796.089--dc23

CONTENTS

CHAPTER ONE

BARRIER BREAKER

O n July 11, 1957, the sun shone brightly over Battery Park in New York City. A 29-year-old woman sat on top of the back seat of a long, sleek convertible. A chauffeur guided the car slowly down Broadway and toward City Hall. More than 100,000 people lined the route, cheering loudly and throwing ticker tape in celebration.[1] The woman they had come to see was history-making tennis player Althea Gibson.

Just two days earlier, Gibson had returned from London, England, after winning the Ladies' Singles championship at Wimbledon. Gibson was the first black athlete—male or female—to win a Wimbledon title. As the victorious Gibson made her way down the parade route, she waved and blew kisses to her fans. When Gibson reached City Hall, the mayor presented her with a medallion of the city.

For Gibson, it was a triumphant homecoming. "I didn't think a Negro girl could go that high," said Gibson's mother, Annie, upon hearing of her daughter's Wimbledon win.[2] It was a common attitude. Being poor, black, and female presented Gibson with sizable challenges. No other woman with a background like Gibson's had reached the highest level of any sport.

BREAKING THE COLOR BARRIER

Although Gibson beamed proudly at the parade, the years it took to get there had been filled with obstacles. Her victory came at a time when ideas about race divided the nation. Like many organizations of the time, tennis clubs were sharply divided along color lines. Gibson got her start at a black tennis club in Harlem called the Cosmopolitan. She played in tournaments sponsored by the American Tennis Association (ATA). It was a league for black tennis players.

FEMALE ATHLETES

Through much of the 1900s, female athletes—regardless of color—faced a number of obstacles. Few organized sports teams existed for girls. If a girl wanted to play sports competitively, often her only option was to join a boys' team. High school athletes were often limited to cheerleading or drill teams. Adult women played sports that were considered socially acceptable, such as tennis, croquet, bowling, and archery. Women who ignored those unwritten rules often found themselves branded as unfeminine.

Gibson's skill and determination made her a standout on the court. But she had little real competition among ATA players. Gibson wanted to face more challenging opponents—white opponents—in major tournaments. She set her sights on the US Nationals, a prestigious tournament now known as the US Open. The problem was that the tournament was run by a whites-only league called the US Lawn Tennis Association (USLTA).

Gibson waves to the crowd as the parade in her honor heads up Broadway in Manhattan.

That obstacle may have seemed impossible to overcome at one time. But society was changing. In 1947, Jackie Robinson had become the first black player in Major League Baseball. Now, three years later, ATA leaders hoped Gibson might be the player to break the color barrier in tennis. "They felt that the time was right, historically, and they felt that in me they had the key they had been looking for to open the door," recalled Gibson. "They hadn't wanted to kick up a fuss until they knew they had a player good enough to back up their argument."[3]

The USLTA hotly debated Gibson's request to play in the tournament. The league ultimately decided she could play in the 1950 US Championships. Gibson lost in the second round. But the experience fueled her desire to play in the best competitions. She continued playing in other prominent tournaments, breaking the color barrier in each one. In 1956, Gibson became the first woman of color to win the singles title at the French Championships. The next year she accomplished the same feat at Wimbledon and the US Championships.

PRO GOLFER

Althea Gibson retired from tennis in 1958. At the time, tennis was exclusively an amateur sport, so players did not earn prize money for their victories. Gibson turned her attention to other pursuits, including professional golf. It was a sport where she could earn money for her efforts. In 1963, Gibson became the first African American in the Ladies Professional Golf Association (LPGA). Though she didn't win any championships as a pro golfer, she had broken a second color barrier in sports.

Gibson lines up a putt during a tournament in 1966.

THE WORK CONTINUES

Gibson's widely publicized victories—both in tennis and in golf, a sport in which she also competed professionally—exposed Americans to what a female athlete of color could achieve. Before Gibson, few women of color had achieved widespread recognition in sports. But American views on race and gender were changing. Many US laws aimed at ending discrimination based on skin color and gender passed in the 1960s and 1970s. They helped open

"I TRY TO DO THE BEST I CAN ..."

"I have never regarded myself as a crusader, I try to do the best I can in every situation I find myself in, and naturally I'm always glad when something I do turns out to be helpful and important to all Negros—or, for that matter, to all Americans, or maybe only to all tennis players. But I don't consciously beat the drums for any special cause, not even the cause of the Negro in the United States, because I feel our best chance to advance is to prove ourselves as individuals. That way, when you are accepted, you are accepted voluntarily, because people appreciate you and respect you and want you, not because you have been shoved down their throats. This doesn't mean that I'm opposed to the fight for integration of the schools or other movements like that. It simply means that in my own career I try to steer clear of political involvement and make my way as Althea Gibson, private individual. I feel that if I am a worthy person, and if I have something worthwhile to contribute, I will be accepted on my own merits, and that is the way I want it."[4]

—*Althea Gibson in her 1958 biography,* I Always Wanted to Be Somebody

Modern tennis stars such as Serena Williams appreciate the example Gibson set for them.

the door for new generations to continue the work Gibson had started.

In the following years, female athletes of color continued to face what has been termed "double discrimination." It is the combination of racism and sexism. Because of this, they had different experiences than male athletes of color or white female athletes. In their quest for success, female athletes of color often faced rude jokes, racial slurs, lost opportunities, and people who belittled their accomplishments.

While the journey has not been easy, the story is not all despair. It is also filled with dramatic victories. Female athletes of color have risen to prominence as college, professional, and Olympic athletes. But the story is not over yet, and Gibson's example of resilience is still strong. "Althea Gibson paved the way for all women of color in sport," said tennis superstar Serena Williams in a 2016 tweet. "Thank you Althea."[5]

DISCUSSION STARTERS

- How do you think pioneers such as Althea Gibson still influence today's athletes?
- Do you think athletes have a responsibility to call attention to injustices in society? Why or why not?
- In your opinion, has race or gender been a more substantial barrier to female athletes of color?

CHAPTER TWO

LAWS CREATE OPPORTUNITIES

Mamie "Peanut" Johnson was born in Ridgeway, South Carolina, in 1935. She spent her childhood playing sandlot baseball with local boys. Not many girls were interested in playing, but Johnson could not get enough of the game. "I used to dream about playing professional baseball," Johnson recalled. "And then I used to think, 'Hey, I know I can't do this because they won't even let the white boys play with the black boys . . . so no, I'm not going to make it there.'"[1]

At the time, Major League Baseball was segregated and there were no leagues for women. Then a series of events took place that changed this. The United States joined World War II (1939–1945) in 1941. Thousands of young men enlisted in the military, including professional baseball players. In an effort to keep the stands full, baseball team owners created a women's league in 1943. It became known as the All-American Girls Professional Baseball League.

After graduating from high school, Johnson and a friend traveled to Alexandria, Virginia, to try out for the league. At the time, all they knew about the league was that it was professional baseball for women. Neither Johnson nor her friend knew that the league had only white women in it. Equipped with gloves and baseball uniforms, they arrived at tryouts only to receive a cold reception. "They just looked at us, as if to say, 'What do you want?'" recalled Johnson. "They wouldn't give us the opportunity to try out."[2]

The women returned home disappointed. Johnson married, had a son, and worked at an ice cream parlor. She continued to play baseball with men on the weekends. Then one day, a scout from the Negro Leagues arrived at one of her games. Major League Baseball had been integrated. Many of its top players were leaving to play in the majors. Negro League scouts were looking for new talent, and they thought Johnson might be a good fit.

Johnson tried out for the Indianapolis Clowns, and she made the team. She pitched for them from 1953 to 1955. Johnson was one of only three women in the Negro Leagues, and she was the only female pitcher. During her time with the Clowns, she earned the respect of her male teammates and fans alike with a 33–8 record as a pitcher and a .270 batting average.[3]

THE NEGRO LEAGUES AND WOMEN

The Negro Leagues formed in the 1920s, when segregation still existed in baseball. In 1953, one Negro League team, the Indianapolis Clowns, made history by signing Toni "Tomboy" Stone. She was the first woman in history to join a men's professional sports team. Stone played in 50 games during her first season, with a batting average of .243.[4] She retired after two seasons in the league but continued to play amateur baseball for many years.

THE CIVIL RIGHTS MOVEMENT

Around the time Johnson was playing with the Clowns, the civil rights movement began to take on a larger presence throughout the United States. The fight for equal rights under the law for people of color had become a major point of discussion in US society and politics. In theory, all citizens have equal rights under the US Constitution, but in practice this did not happen. The civil rights of people of color were often ignored. This was especially true in the South, where a system of segregation and discrimination known as Jim Crow established the dominance of white Americans over people of color. The civil rights movement sought to end this. Success in this endeavor would help fight one of the two major barriers female athletes of color faced: racism.

The movement's crowning achievement was the Civil Rights Act. It guaranteed equal rights to all US citizens, no matter their race, color, religion, or national origin. It also banned segregation and discrimination in schools and places of employment. The bill sharply divided lawmakers, but Congress ultimately passed it after much debate. On July 2, 1964, President Lyndon B. Johnson signed the Civil Rights Act into law.

The Civil Rights Act was a step in the right direction in the fight against racism. But women still faced another barrier to equal rights: sexism. Women, especially those who were not white, were poorly represented in many fields

Mamie "Peanut" Johnson, who pitched for the Indianapolis Clowns of the Negro Leagues, had a baseball field named after her in Washington, DC, in 2013.

WILMA RUDOLPH'S INFLUENCE

The 1960 Olympics in Rome, Italy, were the first games ever televised internationally. One of the biggest stories was African American track star Wilma Rudolph. She amazed spectators by becoming the first woman to win three gold medals in track and field at a single Olympics. When she returned home, she used her fame to bring attention to the civil rights movement. Her hometown of Clarksville, Tennessee, organized parades and banquets to celebrate Rudolph. But she refused to attend because the events were going to be segregated. Rudolph's influence persuaded city leaders to change their plans. The celebration for Rudolph was the city's first integrated public event.

from academics to sports. Sexism was still very much alive and legal. It would take another decade, another landmark law, and the momentum of the women's movement before women of color had any chance at true equality.

TITLE IX

The most successful law to address gender discrimination was called Title IX—Prohibition of Sex Discrimination. President Richard Nixon signed it into law on June 23, 1972. It stated: "No person in the United States shall, on the basis of sex, be excluded from participation in, be denied the benefits of, or be subjected to discrimination under any education program or activity receiving Federal financial assistance."[5] Schools had six years to prepare for the changes, which would take effect on July 21, 1978.

In essence, the goal of Title IX was to correct inequalities in the way male and female students were treated in schools. Before Title IX, many colleges used quotas to determine how many women could be admitted each year. For example, for every 100 men admitted, the college might allow only 20 women. In many cases, female applicants also had to have higher grades and test scores than their male peers to be admitted to a college.

Inequalities between the genders extended to school sports as well. Researcher Margaret Dunkle provided much of the background information to support Title IX. She found, for example, that some universities provided male athletes, but not female athletes, with access to doctors and insurance. At another school, Dunkle discovered that the women's varsity basketball players had access to the gym only when the men's team did not want it. Men's teams also benefited from much larger budgets. Most female teams had to rely on fund-raising and donations.

PATSY TAKEMOTO MINK

Patsy Takemoto Mink is often dubbed the mother of Title IX. Mink was a Japanese American attorney from Hawaii. She served in the US House of Representatives from 1965 to 1977 and then again from 1990 to 2002. Mink was the first woman of color to serve as a US representative. She focused her efforts on civil rights and women's rights. Mink was the principal author of Title IX.

Title IX launched a vast expansion of women's sports in the 1970s.

THE IMPACT

More than 40 years later, Title IX's impact is remarkable. Female high school and college graduation rates have risen steadily. This boom in education has allowed women to enter the workforce in larger numbers and earn higher wages than at any other time in history.

While these achievements are impressive, Title IX's biggest impact has taken place on courts and fields and in gyms. The law required that opportunities to play sports be equal between male and female students. If a school offered ten varsity sports to male athletes, it had to offer ten varsity sports to female athletes, too. The sports themselves could be different, as could the funding available to each sport. It was the number of opportunities that was the key part of the law.

As schools came into compliance with Title IX, women took advantage of the new sports opportunities in droves. In the 1971–72 school year, approximately 300,000 women participated in high school sports. By the 2013–14 school year, that number had risen to 3.2 million—an increase of more than 1,000 percent. In contrast, the participation of male high school athletes during the same time period rose by only 23 percent.[6]

These increasing percentages of female athletes are impressive at first glance. But while Title IX made major improvements, problems still existed. Racism and sexism, though banned in theory, still existed in practice. The double blow of these lingering beliefs widened the gap in sports participation between female athletes of color and their white counterparts.

DISCUSSION STARTERS

- Do you know anyone for whom Title IX has made a difference? If so, in what way did the law change their lives?
- Do you think schools should have to cut back on boys' sports to comply with Title IX? Why or why not?
- Do you think women should be allowed to play on men's professional teams? Why or why not?

CHAPTER THREE

BARRIERS

When thinking back on the game he loves, soccer coach Doug Andreassen sees problems. Most of them have to do with the process of discovering some of the nation's best young players. Andreassen served as the chairman of US Soccer's diversity task force. In a 2016 interview, he revealed that he keeps in mind one soccer player in particular. She was a phenomenal 15-year-old whose future disappeared just as suddenly as it had arrived.

The girl was the daughter of Mexican immigrants. She had grown up playing soccer with her brothers. During that time, she had developed amazing soccer skills. Local coaches wanted her to a play at an Olympic Development tournament. It was out of state, and she could not afford to go. The coaches were so adamant that she attend, they found sponsors to pay for her trip.

The girl played amazingly well at the tournament. College coaches who had watched her play in the tournament were blown away. She received several offers to play in college, a rare feat for such a young soccer player. That's why her local coaches were stunned to learn that she quit playing soccer shortly after returning home.

When they dug into the matter, they quickly learned why she quit. The girl's father was an undocumented immigrant. He feared any attention his daughter received might lead authorities to realize his status and deport him. No one at the soccer league ever saw the standout player again.

BY THE NUMBERS

The barrier this soccer player faced was just one of many that girls of color experience in sports. Researchers want to know Title IX's effects on all female athletes—not just white women. A 2008 study commissioned by the National Women's Sports Foundation looked at participation in sports by gender and race. The survey looked at students in grades three through 12. Results showed that the majority of female athletes—60 percent— were white. Hispanic girls accounted for 17 percent, African American girls 15 percent, and Asian American girls 8 percent.[1]

Recently, experts have begun to study how race and gender intersect to affect

BOSTON SHOWSTOPPERS

Community groups are helping to break barriers to sports for girls of color. One of those programs is the Boston Showstoppers. This nonprofit basketball organization began with seven girls in 2007. Today, it has more than 150 girls between the ages of seven and 18. The girls have won many elite tournaments. They also have impressive school records. Since 2013, the program's players have graduated from high school at a rate of 100 percent.[2] More than half of those girls have gone on to play college basketball.

Olympic gold medalist Benita Fitzgerald Mosley has been an advocate of expanding athletic opportunities for girls and women of color.

sports participation. It is an area that has been studied relatively little. In the past, when researchers studied sports participation they studied either race or gender, but not both at once. That is changing as people consider both factors that affect the experiences of female athletes.

While the participation gap has existed for decades, it is just beginning to get attention. Benita Fitzgerald Mosley, who won Olympic gold in the 100-meter hurdles event in 1984, commented on how much work is left to close the gap. "There's a lot to celebrate," said Fitzgerald Mosley. "There's a whole host of African American women who have benefited greatly from Title IX. We've gotten college scholarships and college degrees; we've made Olympic teams. . . . But in the grand scheme of things, Caucasian girls have benefited disproportionately well, especially suburban girls and wealthy Caucasian girls."[3]

This leads to another question: What is keeping women of color from participating in sports at levels equal to their white peers? It's a complex question with no easy answers. For some girls, the barrier is their neighborhood. They may have no places near their homes to play sports safely. For other girls, it has more to do with their families. They need to spend their free time helping out with cooking, cleaning, and doing part-time work. They cannot spend any time on sports. And then there is the cost. As schools raise the cost to play sports, many girls of color are left out of the game.

But the story is not all negative. Many community organizations are working to provide girls of color with opportunities to play sports. And those opportunities are influencing their lives in ways they never imagined.

NEIGHBORHOOD BARRIERS

While girls have fewer opportunities to play school sports, pickup games after school or on weekends are still an option. However, many girls of color are not doing this. A Centers for Disease Control and Prevention study revealed that girls of color are less likely than white girls to get at least 60 minutes of physical activity per week.[4] This leads to a number of problems, including obesity and poor body image.

One reason for this gap in activity levels has to do with neighborhoods. They directly influence how much time children spend outdoors being active. Heavy traffic and high levels of crime deter children from going outside for fun. According to the US Census Bureau, 87 percent of white respondents believed that they had safe areas for children to play in their neighborhoods. The numbers were much lower for families of color. Only 68 percent of Hispanics and 71 percent of African Americans believed their children had safe places to play.[5]

Additionally, the neighborhoods where girls of color live are more likely to be urban areas with fewer green

Playgrounds and other sports facilities in urban settings often are substandard compared to those in suburbs or small towns.

spaces in total. Green spaces include parks, trails, and other outdoor recreational spaces. They also include other local sports facilities, such as pools, golf courses, tennis courts, and ice arenas. For a girl to reach safe and well-maintained facilities often requires her to leave the neighborhood. In turn, this means she needs transportation. For many girls, this is yet another barrier.

Getting to sporting sites that are not within walking distance or accessible by public transportation is not easy

TRANSIT TO TRAILS

In an effort to make access to natural areas easier, many cities are experimenting with transit-to-trail programs. A program in Los Angeles, California, provides mass transit from inner-city areas to the San Gabriel Mountains. Though Latinos and Asians make up 75 percent of the nearby population, these groups make up only 16 percent of visitors to the park. Community leaders hope the transit-to-trail program will change this. Nelson Trujillo, a local resident, was excited about the program. "There is no safe place for outdoor recreation where I live. It's dangerous," said Trujillo. "I think physical activity will improve the health of my children, keep them safe, healthy and out of trouble."[6]

for many girls of color. Parents who work long hours may not have the ability to drive their daughters to far-off facilities. The cost of transportation to games and tournaments out of state is even more staggering. For many girls, the lack of convenient and affordable transportation is a game ender.

THE FAMILY'S IMPACT

The issue of barriers to playing sports becomes more complex when family influence is added. Girls of color may find that their family situation is another barrier to sports. It is directly connected to the role a girl is often expected to play within the family. Girls who live in low-income or immigrant families are more likely to have many family responsibilities when compared with those who grow up experiencing greater economic privilege. This may include caring for younger siblings, making dinner, or taking a part-time job. The lack of free time means sports often get overlooked.

Even if a girl is able to carve out the time needed to play sports, she may not get support from her family. Some parents hold on to the traditional idea that sports are for boys only. Instead, they may encourage their daughters to pursue more traditionally feminine activities, such as cheerleading. These types of attitudes are most common among immigrants and Hispanic families.

Rosa Mendez, an immigrant from Nicaragua whose family settled in Kansas City, Missouri, expressed this idea when talking about her daughter's passion for soccer. "[My daughter] tries very hard, she asks for shoes, she asks for permission to go to practice," said Mendez. "And all she gets is bruises. She gets hurt sometimes. She gets frustrated. I've been to a couple of games and she lost, so I said, 'It's not worth it.' You get hurt and you lose. Her dad, he feels the same way. But she says: 'I like it.'"[7]

THE COST OF SPORTS

Some families may also lack the financial resources to make playing sports a reality for their girls. The cost of playing a school sport can add up quickly. As governments have been providing less economic support for public schools, schools have begun to charge students to play. Sixty-one percent of American middle and high schools charge a pay-to-play

The costs for training and participation in youth sports can prevent some families from taking part.

fee. On top of the fee, families are responsible for the cost of equipment, uniforms, and other expenses. In 2012, the average American family paid $381 per child to play one season of a sport. In traveling or elite leagues, the price tag can reach into the thousands of dollars.[8]

While scholarships are available, they come with their own problems, including pressure from the parents of the other players who help fund the scholarships. "[They] will say to scholarship kids—and I have seen this countless times—'Why did you miss the game on Saturday? We are paying for you to be here,'" said Nick Lusson of NorCal Premier Soccer Foundation, a group that facilitates opportunities to play soccer for Northern California's underserved communities. "What does a kid say to that? Or what happens if they are late to practice? Or who is going to pay for them to travel to that tournament in San Diego? That's like the moon to some of these kids. We have kids here in the East Bay who have never seen the beach."[9]

Despite the many barriers, girls of color do play sports. While some play for fun, others want to become professional athletes. The opportunities for these girls are slowly starting to grow. Girls growing up today can look to a number of role models. From boxing to figure skating, women of color are making their mark on the world of sports.

DISCUSSION STARTERS

o What do you think are the most difficult barriers women of color face when it comes to playing sports?

o Have you or someone you know been kept from playing sports because of pay-to-play fees? How does that make you feel?

o In what ways do you think families can increase sports participation for girls of color?

CHAPTER FOUR

YOUTH AND COLLEGE SPORTS

G etting girls involved in youth sports at an early age is an important factor in developing a lifelong love of athletics. For this to happen, sports must be accessible, affordable, and socially accepted. They also must be fun. Athletes are more likely to continue in sports if they enjoy themselves and have good experiences. The benefits that come from sports can change the entire course of a girl's life in a positive way.

The health benefits of playing youth sports are enormous. Female athletes have lower levels of breast cancer, osteoporosis, and depression. Sports also keep the body fit, which is important with the rising levels of childhood obesity. The rate of obesity among high school students is highest among African American and Hispanic girls. Playing sports can reduce this risk. According to research, women who played sports as children had a 7 percent lower rate of obesity 20 to 25 years later. No other public health program has a success rate that high.[1]

Playing youth sports is also linked to a lower willingness among girls to take social risks such as drinking or having unprotected sex. African American and Hispanic teenage girls are twice as likely to get pregnant as their white peers.[2] Girls who participate in high school and college sports are

Studies have shown that female athletes tend to excel in the classroom as well.

MO'NE DAVIS

Girls of color are smashing all kinds of barriers in youth sports—and gaining national media attention for doing it. Mo'ne Davis of Philadelphia, Pennsylvania, is one of the most prominent leaders in this arena. In 2014, Davis made headlines in the Little League World Series (LLWS). She was the eighteenth girl in history to play in the LLWS and the first girl ever to pitch a shutout at the tournament. Teammate Jahli Hendricks said, "I've heard players say, 'I got struck out by a girl!' They are pretty amazed by her. We are, too, but it's not because she's a girl. It's because she's a great pitcher."[4]

significantly less likely to become pregnant. Female athletes are also less likely to engage in other risky behaviors, such as drinking, smoking, and doing drugs.

Academic success, especially as it relates to high school graduation rates, is closely related to playing sports. The dropout rate among American girls in 2010 was 22 percent.[3] This rate was significantly higher among girls of color. Girls of color who played sports, however, were less likely to fall into this category. They had better grades, higher scores on standardized tests, and a higher likelihood of graduating.

Female athletes are also more likely to participate in the workforce, especially in traditionally male-dominated fields such as engineering and finance. A 2010 study that analyzed employment data found that the wages of women who played sports in high school were 11 to 14 percent higher than their nonathletic counterparts. This wage increase was after taking into account age, race, and family background. The study also found that more than four out of five female executives had played sports growing up.[5]

YOUTH SPORTS

Given the multitude of benefits sports provide, encouraging girls to play can have a positive impact on their lives for years. But not all girls have equal access to youth sports. A 2015 study by the National Women's Law Center found that a girl's biggest barrier to sports had to do with the school she attends. A girl who attends a heavily minority school has fewer athletic opportunities than a girl who attends a heavily white school. The study defined a heavily white school as one with a student population that was 90 percent white. Likewise, a heavily minority school was defined as one with 90 percent students of color. In the United States, 42 percent of high schools fall into one of these two categories.[6]

While participation levels between girls and boys differ in both types of school, the disparity is greatest in heavily minority schools. An average minority school has only 20 team spots available for every 100 girls enrolled. In contrast, for every 100 boys enrolled at a minority school, 30 team spots are available. This means girls at a typical minority school have only 67 percent of the opportunities to play sports that boys have.[7]

This gender-based difference is what researchers call an opportunity gap. Some level of opportunity gap exists in nearly all schools. A heavily minority school is twice as likely to have a large opportunity gap as is a heavily white school.[8] In practical terms, this means that girls in heavily minority schools have fewer chances to play sports. It also means that schools are not complying with Title IX.

The report also noted that Alabama, Mississippi, and North Carolina had the largest number of schools with opportunity gaps in the country. "States that fell to the bottom of the ranking of our report also have larger populations of people of color," said Katherine Gallagher Robbins, who works for the National Women's Law Center. "That's part of the overall story and part of the untold story of Title IX."[9]

COLLEGE ATHLETES

Despite the barriers, the number of female athletes participating in college athletics has risen dramatically since Title IX.

TITLE IX COMPLIANCE

The Office for Civil Rights is a part of the US Department of Education. It enforces federal civil rights laws in schools and related activities. These laws apply to any school that receives federal funding. If students believe their school is not in compliance with Title IX or any other civil rights laws, they can file a complaint with this office. The agency has 12 enforcement branches across the nation. The agents work to prevent, identify, and end discrimination practices in American schools.

But studies have also shown that the majority of these athletes are white women. During the 2015–16 school year, 72.6 percent of female college athletes were white. The remaining female student-athletes were 9.3 percent African American, 5.2 percent Latina, 2.5 percent Asian American, and 0.4 percent Native American. The remaining female athletes identified as two or more races or were nonresident aliens.[10]

This disparity was the topic of many conversations when Title IX celebrated its fortieth anniversary in 2012. Tina Sloan Green was one of the more outspoken people about this issue. Green became the country's first female African American head coach in women's lacrosse while working at Temple University. She was also a cofounder and president of the organization Black Women in Sport. Green believes the gap is intentional and that racism and greed are

BASKETBALL AND TRACK

Female athletes of color are unequally represented across college sports. At Division I schools in 2016–17, African Americans made up 43.4 percent of women's basketball players.[11] African Americans made up 24 percent of women's Division I track teams.[12] Many other sports—swimming, lacrosse, golf, skiing, rugby—have single-digit participation levels for women of color. This concentration in two sports reduces opportunities. Athletes are competing for a small number of team spots and scholarships. It shuts out all but the most elite athletes. In contrast, white female athletes are spread more equally across a larger variety of sports. This opens up more opportunities, giving white female athletes more chances to participate.

University of South Carolina head coach Dawn Staley calls out instructions to her players at a women's basketball game in 2018.

at its core. "These white women don't want us to compete with them. They want their kids to get the scholarships. They're thinking about themselves," said Green. "They give us all kinds of awards, but when it comes time to distributing the money, it's a whole other story."[13]

It's not just student athletes who face an uneven playing field in college sports. Coaches and administrators are also predominantly white. In women's basketball, for example, women of color make up only 10.9 percent of college coaches. This does not represent the makeup of college basketball teams, where African American women make up 45.4 percent of rosters.[14] The numbers are even more dismal in sports where women of color are not as well represented, such as swimming, golf, and lacrosse.

In 2015, the National Collegiate Athletic Association (NCAA) released a report on its study of barriers to women of color in leadership positions within college sports. According to the report, women of color represent less than 7 percent of all college coaches or athletic administrators.[15] The 529 women of color who took part in the study all worked in athletics administration or coaching. They identified major barriers to taking sports leadership positions. Many respondents cited the lack of role models in these positions as a barrier. Others believed it had to do with a lack of available positions, as well as stereotypes about women in sports.

DISCUSSION STARTERS

o Why do you think youth and college sports have more white female participants?

o What would you do to increase participation rates for girls and women of color in youth and college sports?

o How do you think coaches and administrators affect female participation in sports?

CHAPTER FIVE

OLYMPIANS

I n 1896, French aristocrat Baron Pierre de Coubertin established the modern Olympic Games. Female athletes were not given a seat at the table. "I am personally against the participation of women in public competitions," wrote Coubertin. He said that Olympic Games should be the "solemn and periodic exaltation of male athleticism with internationalism as a base, loyalties as a means, arts for its setting, and female applause as reward."[1]

Fortunately, Coubertin was not the last word on women in the Olympics. More than 100 years after the modern games started, women of all backgrounds and ethnicities have had the opportunity to compete. It did not happen overnight, though. The 2012 Olympics in London, England, marked the first time all participating nations sent female athletes to the games.

Until that point, Qatar, Brunei, and Saudi Arabia were the only countries that had never sent women to the games. All three nations changed that statistic during the 2012 games. Bahiya Al-Hamad of Qatar competed in the air rifle event and said of her Olympic appearance, "It's an accomplishment for every Qatari woman."[2]

American athletes did not have to wait nearly as long as Al-Hamad did to participate. At the 1900 games in Paris,

France, women were allowed to participate in five events: tennis, golf, croquet, yachting, and equestrian events. American Margaret Abbott signed up for an amateur golf tournament while studying in France. She won the competition, at which point she received a porcelain bowl surrounded by gold. Then she went home, having no idea that she had become the first American woman to win an Olympic gold medal.

For black women, the opportunity to win Olympic medals came later still. The 1948 Summer Olympics in London represented a major breakthrough. Audrey Patterson earned a bronze in the 200-meter sprint to become the first African American woman to win an Olympic medal. Her teammate, Alice Coachman, won the high jump. She was the first African American woman to win a gold medal. Patterson and Coachman were just the beginning

OLYMPICS AND RACE

For some people, the Olympics are a two-week celebration of diversity and equality on the sports field. But some people criticize the media for presenting an idealized picture of race in the United States. "The efforts to reframe the Games as evidence of racial reconciliation and post-raciality embodies the ways that we want to wash racism away," explained David Leonard, a professor from Washington State University who studies gender, race, and culture. "White America has always used the Olympics as a way to stage a particular racial vision of itself and the 2016 Games have been no different."[3]

of an amazing legacy of female athletes of color in the Olympic games.

DOMINATING IN RIO

At the 2016 Games in Rio de Janeiro, Brazil, 558 athletes represented Team USA. Women made up more than half of the athletes on the American team.[4] People of color made up 23 percent of the team.[5] As the games progressed, female athletes of color began to dominate the medal podiums across a wide variety of events. "It is very interesting to see black women going into areas where you really don't see black women competing, with all different body shapes, complexion, and hairstyles being represented," said Kaye Wise Whitehead, a professor of race and gender studies at Maryland's Loyola University. "Black women see and feel that there is no door closed to us . . . and that we're not just walking through those doors, but we're dominating."[6]

One of many notable athletes during the Rio games was swimmer Simone Manuel. Her victory in the 100-meter freestyle made her the first African American female to win an individual gold medal in swimming. The medal was especially poignant. That's because during segregation African Americans were not allowed into whites-only swimming pools. As a result, few learned to swim, and the legacy continues to this day. According to one 2017 study,

Swimmer Simone Manuel was one of the many outstanding female athletes competing for Team USA in the 2016 Olympics.

64 percent of African American children do not know how to swim.[7]

Manuel addressed these historic challenges and her hope for the future in a 2017 open letter. "I am often referred to as 'The Black Swimmer.' While I one day hope to be known as an 'Olympic champion' swimmer without that

SWIMMING AFTER DESEGREGATION

The relationship between African Americans and swimming remained treacherous even after desegregation. "When I was growing up, we all heard about the black kids who got beat up or held underwater if they tried to go to public pools," said Ebony Rosemond, founder of the website BlackKidsSwim.com. "People threw stones at black kids who went to the beach. There is this legacy of fear that got to be associated with swimming, and it wasn't just about drowning. It was also about being attacked and driven away."[9]

In the years immediately following the passage of the Civil Rights Act, some cities had workers fill in their municipal pools with concrete rather than desegregate them. At hotel pools, if an African American so much as dipped a toe in the water, white patrons could demand the pool be drained, cleaned, and refilled. Some white workers went so far as to pour acid in the pool water if they saw an African American patron swimming. These days, those drastic actions might seem like they took place in some bygone era. But it's another reminder that today's society is only a generation or two removed from the days of rampant segregation.

qualifier, I know that I can't ignore the significance of being an African American female in the sport. . . . There are more African American swimmers than when I first started in the sport and if we want more diversity in the water, it starts with learning how to swim."[8]

Like Manuel, other women of color on Team USA chalked up a number of firsts. The women's gymnastics team had more minorities than white members for the first time in US history. Likewise, for the first time in history all four athletes on the US women's tennis team were African American. Goalie Ashleigh Johnson became the first African

52

American woman to represent Team USA in water polo. And these are just the most publicized examples. Women of color represented Team USA in track and field, boxing, tae kwon do, weight lifting, basketball, and rugby.

Back in the United States, fan Andrea Lawful-Sanders cheered on women of color in the Olympics from her home in Philadelphia, Pennsylvania. "While everybody else is talking, we are doing," said Lawful-Sanders. "When we excel, nobody can take that away from us—ever. They may try to marginalize us, but how can you marginalize excellence? . . . It's black girl magic. We are tired of being told that we couldn't or we shouldn't. . . . We're taking no prisoners, and I'm enjoying every second of it."[10]

REWRITING HISTORY IN PYEONGCHANG

The Rio Olympics had been a great success for Team USA in general, and

IBTIHAJ MUHAMMAD

In the 2016 games, fencer Ibtihaj Muhammad became the first American athlete in the Olympic games to wear a head scarf called a hijab. Muhammad began fencing because it was a sport that allowed her to keep her head and body covered, an important part of her faith as a Muslim. Though she did not win any individual medals in the Olympics, Muhammad's presence was influential. "It almost seems to be this trending thing, where our girls are being told that there's things that they can't do or shouldn't do," said Muhammad. "And it's not necessarily specific to Muslim girls. I would say there are tons of girls out there who find inspiration in my story regardless of their faith and are becoming more involved in sport."[11]

Snowboarder Chloe Kim had a breakout performance for Team USA in the 2018 Olympics in PyeongChang, South Korea.

for female athletes of color in particular. Two years later, in PyeongChang, South Korea, American athletes again smashed barriers and made history. Team USA brought 243 athletes to the Winter Olympics in PyeongChang, making it the largest team at the Games. Despite this, the team's diversity was lacking. Of all the athletes, only 10 were African American and 10 were Asian American. The rest were white.

The lack of diversity in the Winter Olympics is neither new nor unique to Team USA. The reason for this has to do with the types of sports featured in the Winter Games. Many of the sports require special training facilities that are located in only a few places across the country. The costs to participate can also limit who plays winter sports. Athletes have to pay for expensive lift tickets, ice time, and equipment. Given the scarcity of training facilities, travel expenses also figure into the cost to play.

To work toward more diverse teams, in 2012 the US Olympic Committee (USOC) created a position called the director of diversity and inclusion. Jason Thompson was the first person to fill this position. His goal is to create more diversity in all aspects of Team USA, including athletes, coaches, officials, and administrators. "We've just been trying to find ways to make sure our team looks like America," said Thompson.[12] That effort will take time to bear fruit. Researchers estimate that it takes an average of

RACE AND ENDORSEMENTS

For many Olympic athletes, their goals are twofold: to win their event and also secure endorsements. Endorsements are an important source of income for athletes who cannot earn a living by competing in their sport. Historically, these multimillion-dollar endorsements have been given to attractive white women, such as alpine skiers Lindsey Vonn and Mikaela Shiffrin. As the diversity increases on Team USA, the endorsements are slowly changing, too. Most notably, after the 2018 games, Chloe Kim landed a number of major endorsements, including campaigns for Nike, Burton, Toyota, Visa, Samsung, and Monster Energy.

eight to ten years of intense training for an athlete to reach elite status.[13]

Though their numbers were small, the female athletes of color in the 2018 PyeongChang Games made history. Snowboarder Chloe Kim dazzled on the half-pipe with back-to-back 1080s, making three full revolutions in midair on consecutive jumps. This feat had never been done at the Olympics, and it won her the gold medal. Figure skater Mirai Nagasu became the first American woman to land a triple axel—three and one-half revolutions from a forward takeoff—at the Olympics. And two African American women—Maame Biney and Erin Jackson—qualified for the US speed skating team, the first time in history that team included more than one African American woman.

These athletes represent a new and more diverse face for female athletes in the Olympics, today and in the future. "You might have a young black girl watching these Winter Olympic sports thinking, 'Well, there's not anyone like me out there. I don't know if there's a place for me in these sports,'" said Jackson. "But I'm looking forward to being in the Winter Olympics and showing, OK, we do have some representation in these sports."[14]

DISCUSSION STARTERS

o   In what ways do you see Olympic teams representing race and gender relations in their countries?

o   If you ran the US Olympic team, what would you do to create more diversity, especially in winter sports?

o   How do you think history impacts the Olympic sports in which athletes excel?

CHAPTER
SIX

THE
PROS

A s Title IX created opportunities for large numbers of female athletes, the need for professional women's sports leagues began to grow. Most of these leagues had a rocky start, disbanding shortly after their creation. Today, professional leagues successfully support female athletes in a number of sports, including basketball, soccer, tennis, and golf.

One of the most visible success stories involves the Women's National Basketball Association (WNBA). In 1996, leaders of the National Basketball Association (NBA) approved a new league of eight women's professional basketball teams. During its inaugural season in the summer of 1997, more than 50 million viewers tuned in to watch WNBA games.[1] Over the following years, the league continued to grow, and as of 2018 it had 12 teams in two divisions. It has become the most successful professional women's sports league in history.

The WNBA is consistently praised for its diversity in players, coaches, managers, trainers, and executives. Each year the Institute for Diversity and Ethics in Sport (TIDES) grades sports teams on their levels of diversity. In 2017, the WNBA earned a combined grade of A for race and gender hiring practices. "The WNBA continues to lead the way in terms of racial and gender diversity amongst all professional leagues," said Richard Lapchick, the director of TIDES. "The WNBA again received the highest number of A's as well as the lowest number of grades below an A in all categories compared to men's professional leagues."[2]

The 2017 diversity numbers the WNBA put up are impressive. African American women made up 68.5 percent of league players. White women constituted 24.5 percent, Latinas 3.5 percent, and 2.8 percent were listed as "other." The league also included one Asian American player and 16.2 percent international players.[3]

One area in which the WNBA falls short is player salaries. The average salary in the WNBA is $50,000, and salaries top out at $110,000. In the NBA, however, the average starting salary is

POWERFUL WOMEN IN SPORTS

For years, professional sports have been dominated by men—not only on the field but in team offices as well. That is slowly starting to change. Women from a wide variety of backgrounds are taking positions of power with professional teams. In a list of most-powerful women in sports combined by *Forbes* magazine, Michelle Roberts topped the list. The African American lawyer became the executive director of the National Basketball Players Association in 2014. It made her the first woman to lead a professional sports union. In her position, Roberts represents 350 NBA players and handles $3 billion in player salaries.[4]

Nneka Ogwumike is one of the many WNBA stars who get paid much less than their male counterparts in the NBA.

$560,000, and a maximum contract is worth more per year than the WNBA's entire salary budget. To put it into further perspective, Stephen Curry, the NBA Most Valuable Player (MVP) in 2016, made more than $34 million in 2017–18.[5] Meanwhile, the WNBA's maximum salary is $110,000, less than 20 percent of the *average starting salary* of an NBA player.[6]

Nneka Ogwumike, the 2016 WNBA MVP, and many of her fellow players must play overseas or take other side jobs in the off-season to reach their full earning potential. "I feel like we have a lot of work to do," she said.

Player salaries are based on team revenue. Getting more fans in the stands and more lucrative television contracts could go a long way toward meeting this goal. "Once you get more eyes on us, more ears on us, it'll bring more business

SPORTS AND ACTIVISM

Like players in a variety of sports, the athletes of the WNBA have used their visibility to draw attention to causes important to them. In the 2016 season, several players were fined for wearing T-shirts that showed their support for the Black Lives Matter movement during pregame warm-ups. To protest the fines, the players refused to talk to reporters about anything related to the game. Instead, they used their airtime to talk about racially motivated violence in African American communities. In the 2017 season, many players locked arms or took a knee during the national anthem to protest violence against people of color. "If TIDES was to give a grade for athlete activism the WNBA players would get an unquestionable A+," said Lapchick.[7]

and more private entities that help support us," noted
Ogwumike.[8]

SOCCER

In the spring of 2013, the US Soccer Federation launched
a professional women's league: the National Women's
Soccer League (NWSL). It was a risky proposition. Two other
women's professional soccer leagues had failed in the past,
largely because they could not generate enough revenue.
The NWSL seems to have solved this problem, but it is
still hard at work conquering another problem: diversity.
Traditionally, American women's soccer has been criticized
for being a sport of white suburbanites. On average, about
three-quarters of NWSL players have been white. That is
slowly beginning to change, though.

In the NWSL's 2017 draft, half of the first-round players
selected were women of color. "It's exciting that there's
so many women of color," said Ifeoma Onumonu, who
was drafted eighth by the Boston Breakers. "Half of the
first-round picks being women of color just shows this
sport's expanding. It's becoming popular. People are
becoming more open to it."[9]

It will take time for the diversity to grow in the NWSL.
Part of that has do with the types of messages women
of color receive about where they belong in the sporting
world. "Even when I was growing up, I was pushed into

Ifeoma Onumonu, left, makes a play in a 2018 NWSL match.

certain sports . . . mostly track, which is supposed to be—
it's a predominantly African American sport, especially
for women," Onumonu recalled.[10] Crystal Dunn, another
player in the NWSL, recalled facing limited views of the skills
African American women brought to soccer. "I think there's
so many stereotypes about black women playing soccer,
[that] all they are is fast," said Dunn.[11]

While the color barrier is breaking down in women's
soccer, salaries are still an area of contention. NWSL players,
like their peers in the WNBA, often struggle to earn enough

money to support themselves as professional athletes. League salaries range from $15,750 to $44,000 per year.[12] In contrast, the men's professional soccer league in the United States—Major League Soccer—pays its players a minimum of $70,250.[13]

Low salaries have forced some professional women's players out of the game. Jazmine Reeves was a top rookie with the Boston Breakers in 2014, but it didn't translate into a high salary. She earned only $11,000 in her first year, which led her to retire after only one season and take a corporate job that paid better. While Reeves said leaving Boston was difficult, she had no choice. "I'm not saying I would never play again, but I can't live off of what they gave me. I can't," Reeves said.[14]

TENNIS

Unlike soccer and basketball, professional women's tennis players have made strides in earning pay equal to that of their male counterparts. Of the ten highest-paid female athletes of 2017, eight are professional tennis players. While the money is better, the diversity is not. It is still a sport predominantly led by white players.

This is slowly beginning to change, though. Serena Williams, who many experts claim is the greatest women's tennis player of all time, has shattered records across the globe. She is joined in the ranks by her sister Venus Williams,

WORLD'S HIGHEST-PAID FEMALE ATHLETES, 2017[15]

Serena Williams	tennis	$27 million
Angelique Kerber	tennis	$12.6 million
Danica Patrick	auto racing	$12.6 million
Ronda Rousey	mixed martial arts	$11 million
Venus Williams	tennis	$10.5 million
Garbiñe Muguruza	tennis	$7.7 million
Caroline Wozniacki	tennis	$7.5 million
Agnieszka Radwańska	tennis	$7.3 million
Eugenie Bouchard	tennis	$7.1 million
Simona Halep	tennis	$6.2 million

as well as top players Taylor Townsend, Madison Keys, and Sloane Stephens.

However, while the numbers of female athletes of color are increasing, racism is not going away entirely. One of the most high-profile incidents happened to Serena Williams in 2001 at Indian Wells. Serena and Venus were set to play each other in a semifinal match. With four minutes until match time, Venus withdrew, citing a knee injury. Some fans thought it was an attempt to fix the match in Serena's favor. The crowd booed Serena as she took the court. Richard Williams, the girls' father, said that as he and Venus walked to their seats fans shouted racial slurs at them.

While Williams won the tournament, it was a bittersweet victory. "It has been difficult for me to forget spending hours crying in the Indian Wells locker room after winning in

Serena Williams meets with the media upon her return to Indian Wells in 2015.

2001, driving back to Los Angeles feeling as if I had lost the biggest game ever—not a mere tennis game but a bigger fight for equality," she said. Williams refused to play at the Indian Wells tournament for 14 years before she finally ended the boycott.[16]

In the following years, Williams faced a steady stream of racism and sexism. But not all of it was blatant. Microaggressions are a subtler form of discrimination. In 2006, Australian doctor Peter Larkins committed an often-cited microaggression against Williams. In an article, Larkins analyzed the physique and fitness level of several female tennis players. He said of Williams, "It is the African American race. They just have this huge gluteal strength. . . . With Serena, that's her physique and genetics."[17] The comment suggested that Williams is an amazing player because of her African American genes, not because of all the hard work and dedication she puts into her game.

Researchers studied 643 Olympic news stories about Williams and Angelique Kerber, a white tennis player. Researchers discovered 758 microaggressions against Williams but only 18 against Kerber. "We've known for a long time that female athletes often experience discrimination and other microaggressions, but now . . . we have statistical data illustrating this issue," said the study's director, Cynthia Frisby.[18]

GOLF

Like tennis, women's professional golf has traditionally been a white sport. Tennis great Althea Gibson joined the pro golf tour in 1963, breaking the color barrier. Fourteen years later, Nancy Lopez broke another barrier when she became the first Latina on the circuit. Since that time, only six African American women have toured with the Ladies Professional Golf Association (LPGA).

Two of those women, Cheyenne Woods and Sadena Parks, started on the LPGA tour in 2015. "I'd like to help kids think golf is cool, and it's for everybody," said Woods, whose uncle is golf legend Tiger Woods. "But when you look at the LPGA, you don't have a big name of any African American woman who kids can look up to, or put their poster on their wall, or tune in and watch them every week." But Woods and Parks are determined to change that.[19]

To increase diversity in golf, the LPGA created a program called Girls Golf. The program brings the sport to girls who

MICHELLE WIE

Another player making waves in the LPGA is Michelle Wie. Wie was born in Honolulu, Hawaii, in 1989. Her parents were originally from South Korea, but they moved to Hawaii before Wie was born. Wie began playing golf at age 4. By 10, she qualified for a United States Golf Association (USGA) tournament. By age 14, she was playing against men in an event on the PGA circuit. Two years later, Wie turned pro and signed multimillion-dollar contracts with Nike and Sony. She joined the LPGA in 2009 and won the US Open in 2014.

might otherwise not be exposed to the game. For the cost of $10, girls have access to clubs, lessons, and a golf course. Since the program began in 1989, it has introduced more than 300,000 girls to the game. Despite the efforts, only 9 percent of girls who sign up are African American, 9 percent are Latina, and 14 percent are Native American.[20]

The high cost to play golf continues to keep girls out of the game. "Golf is extremely expensive here and kids don't have the lasting support to be able to continue to play for the long term," said Ron Sirak, an award-winning golf journalist. "So while programs like Girls Golf are great, who is going to pay for these girls to keep playing when families can't afford to keep them in the game?"[21]

DISCUSSION STARTERS

- Do you think professional female athletes should receive salaries equal to those of their male counterparts? Why or why not?

- What impact do you think women's professional sports teams have on youth sports for girls?

- Do you think professional athletes can be good role models? What qualities do the best role models have? How can this affect a girl's decision to play sports?

CHAPTER
SEVEN

THE
MEDIA

I n June 2015, a controversial series of tweets about women's sports lit up the internet. The two tweeters—Mark Mravic and Andy Benoit—both worked for *Sports Illustrated*. Mravic began with a tweet calling out Benoit shortly after an especially exciting goal in the FIFA Women's World Cup. Mravic posted video from the Norway vs. England game with this tweet: "And here some people (ahem, @Andy_Benoit) argue that women's soccer isn't worth watching."[1]

Not to be outdone, Benoit responded later with his own tweet that went on to inflame women's sports fans. He wrote, "Not women's soccer . . . women's sports in general not worth watching."[2] Less than an hour later, he attempted to defend his position but ended up making the situation worse: "Women are every bit as good as men in general, better in many aspects, their sports are just less entertaining. TV ratings agree, btw."[3] Eventually, Benoit deleted both posts and the story died.

Just a few months later, though, the topic of women and sports drew the media's attention again. In the fall of 2015, Jessica Mendoza made history by becoming ESPN's first female Major League Baseball (MLB) analyst. Mendoza, an Olympic gold medalist in softball, received positive reviews

Jessica Mendoza became ESPN's first female baseball analyst in 2015.

WHERE ARE THE WOMEN?

Despite all the changes Title IX has created for women's sports, one area that remains dominated by men is sports reporting. Ninety percent of sports editors in the United States are white, and 90 percent are men.[5] While women in general hold only a handful of positions in sports media, women of color are noticeably underrepresented in the industry. That is slowly starting to change, though, as some networks—most notably ESPN—are purposely seeking out ways to diversify their staffs and bring a wider perspective to sports reporting.

from most viewers who were happy to hear a new voice. But not everyone liked having a woman in a traditionally male role.

Mendoza's critics took to social media, spewing a surprising amount of hatred. One high-profile tweeter was Mike Bell, a sports radio host from Atlanta, Georgia. Bell tweeted, "Really? A women's softball slugger as guest analyst on MLB Wildcard Game? Once again ESPN too frigging cute for their own good."[4] Others echoed Bell's comments, with similar remarks that referred to women as annoying and unwelcome in the broadcasting booth.

While these comments are intolerant at best and sexist at worst, they are not new. For years, women's sports and media outlets have been tussling. Battles have centered on the amount and type of coverage women's sports receive. They also extend in other directions, with a push for more female sports reporters on air and in newsrooms. When female athletes of color enter the situation, it expands from just sexism to include blatant expressions of racism.

AMOUNT AND TYPE OF COVERAGE

In the years leading up to Title IX, women's sports received little to no coverage in the media. While some outstanding athletes—Althea Gibson, Wilma Rudolph, and Babe Didrikson, for example—received positive media attention, most coverage focused on men's sports. More than 40 years after the passage of Title IX, little has changed in the media, but much has changed in women's sports.

Today, 40 percent of all participants in American sports are female, but only 4 percent of media coverage focuses on women's sports.[6] This disparity leads to a question: Why doesn't the media cover more women's sports? "I think there is definitely a chicken-and-egg situation here with media and with interest," said Rachel Blount, a sports reporter for the *Star Tribune* of Minneapolis, Minnesota. "I think there is something to the argument that if there were wider media coverage of some [women's] teams and athletes, it would create more interest because more people would be exposed to it."[7]

And yet, even when women's sports are covered by the media, the type of coverage they receive is different from that of men's teams. While the pieces on women's sports are more respectful than in the past, reporters often lack the enthusiasm they have for men's sports stories. And, oftentimes, the accomplishments of female athletes are buried under lifestyle stories about stereotypical female topics—fashion, beauty, and family.

A FOCUS ON APPEARANCES

Given this starting point, it's no surprise that a female athlete's appearance becomes a focus of media interest. Oftentimes, the conversation centers on an athlete's body because it impacts how she performs. This is within the bounds of respectful sports journalism. Olympic reporters, for example, may discuss Simone Biles's four-foot-eight-inch (142 cm) frame, which gives her a strength-to-weight ratio that allows for powerful tumbling passes. That is no different than reporters discussing how Michael Phelps's 80-inch (2 m) arm span and long torso work in his favor to be a good swimmer.

#ASKHERMORE

An organization called the Representation Project actively seeks to challenge the media in the way it portrays stereotypes of gender, race, class, age, religion, and sexual orientation. Its leaders started a social media campaign called #AskHerMore. It calls for reporters to stop asking women about their clothes, makeup, and families and instead focus on their accomplishments. In the 2016 Olympics, the #AskHerMore campaign encouraged people to call out sexist reporting and make the media accountable for how it presents women in athletics.

Olympic gold medalist Gabby Douglas was attacked on social media over her appearance during the 2012 London Games.

For some female athletes of color, however, this type of close analysis crosses the line from sports talk to personal attack. At the 2012 Olympics, gymnast Gabby Douglas found herself at the center of a social media storm that

SEXY OR ATHLETIC?

Many female athletes feel pressure to pose in revealing, sexy photos. Researchers at the Tucker Center for Research on Girls & Women in Sport have studied this phenomenon to figure out why. One theory is that female athletes are blasted with stereotypes about being unfeminine. By posing in a revealing manner, an athlete may feel that she is demonstrating her femininity. Another theory notes that female athletes get less media recognition than males. By posing in revealing ways, women can reclaim some of the missing attention.

centered on her appearance. The 16-year-old had just become the first gymnast in American history to win gold medals in both team and all-around competitions. What many social media users focused on, however, was not her record-breaking achievement. Instead, they were outraged about her hairstyle.

Douglas wore a messy bun—a popular style with young women across the country—with gel and barrettes to keep it in place. The hairstyle looked just like those of all the other gymnasts on her team. That didn't stop social media commenters from saying things like "Why hasn't anyone tried to fix Gabby Douglas's hair?" and "gabby douglas gotta do something with this hair! these clips and this brown gel residue aint it."[8]

Many fans quickly came to the defense of Douglas, directing the conversation back to her achievements. The focus on Douglas has less to do with her hair and more to do with the role of African American women in society.

Professor Tina Opie explained it by saying that many African American women "see hair as a signifier of identity—of class, ethnicity, of gender—it matters. So when these black women see Gabby Douglas wearing her hair in a way they see as sub-par, they view it as a threat, something that will negatively impact how others view them as well. She's a representative of the collective."[9]

RACISM IN COVERAGE

No story displayed the racist and sexist coverage female athletes of color receive quite like what happened with nationally syndicated radio host Don Imus in 2007. That year's National Collegiate Athletic Association (NCAA) women's national championship basketball game pitted the University of Tennessee against the underdogs of Rutgers University. It had been a Cinderella season for the Rutgers team. Despite its low ranking, the team had won the first Big East conference title in the school's history. At the NCAA tournament, Rutgers exploded onto the court and upset Duke, the top overall seed in the tournament. The women's basketball team from Rutgers was poised to win its first national title when the players took court against Tennessee.

The sports media usually loves an underdog story like the one Rutgers provided. But that's not how the 2007 championship will be remembered. Instead, shocking commentary about the players' appearance took center

Rutgers students and faculty members rallied behind their women's basketball team after a radio host criticized the players' appearance.

stage the morning after the game. On his show, which also was televised on MSNBC, Imus and his staff spoke of the Rutgers players in extremely derogatory terms, commenting on their hair and tattoos in ways in which many observers believed they would not speak about white female athletes.

The insensitive banter was broadcast to millions of people across the nation, and it ignited a discussion about how female athletes of color are portrayed in the media.

Rutgers coach C. Vivian Stringer struck back at Imus in a press conference, defending the character of her players who were "valedictorians of their class, future doctors, musical prodigies and, yes, even Girl Scouts. They are all young ladies of class."[10]

Years later, Stringer expanded on her feelings at the time, pointing out the hypocrisy of the media talking about a female athlete's appearance rather than her accomplishments. "I kept reading those words and I was so upset," Stringer said. "I saw this in a lot of different ways. I saw it as racist. But I also saw it as demeaning to women and women's basketball. What difference does someone's hair matter? What major athletic event do you look at a guy and talk about hair or his legs? I kept thinking, 'Why would he say that? He doesn't know us.'"[11]

Imus apologized to Stringer and the Rutgers basketball team, but he still lost his radio show. Meanwhile, the discussion his comments sparked continues.

DISCUSSION STARTERS

- In what ways do you see female athletes in the media influencing girls of color who play sports?
- How do you think sports fans could help change the way female athletes are portrayed in the media?
- Do you think journalists have a responsibility to portray female athletes in a respectful way? Why or why not?

MEDIA
GUIDELINES

The National Women's Sports Foundation created a set of guidelines for reporters to consider when portraying a female athlete in the media. The guidelines seek to create a scenario in which images and news stories about female athletes are treated in the same manner as those representing their male peers. The goal is for coverage to be respectful, fair, and honest.

IMAGES

- Female athletes should be shown in images that represent their skills, not in poses set up for the camera. Their equipment and uniforms should be authentic, not props.

- The image should depict a moment the athlete could feel proud of, not embarrassed by.

- The image should include an athlete's head or face, not just her body.

- The image should be one the woman can be proud of both now and in the future.

WORDS

- The focus of a story on a female athlete should be about her skills or performance, not her appearance.

US gymnast Simone Biles meets with television reporters in 2016.

- Unless the athletes are under age 12, they should be referred to as women, not girls.

- Use words to describe a female athlete and her sport that are equal in tone to men's sports coverage. Avoid words such as "moody," "shapely," and "well-built" and replace them with more neutral counterparts such as "intense," "conditioned," and "physically fit."[12]

CHAPTER EIGHT

THE FUTURE

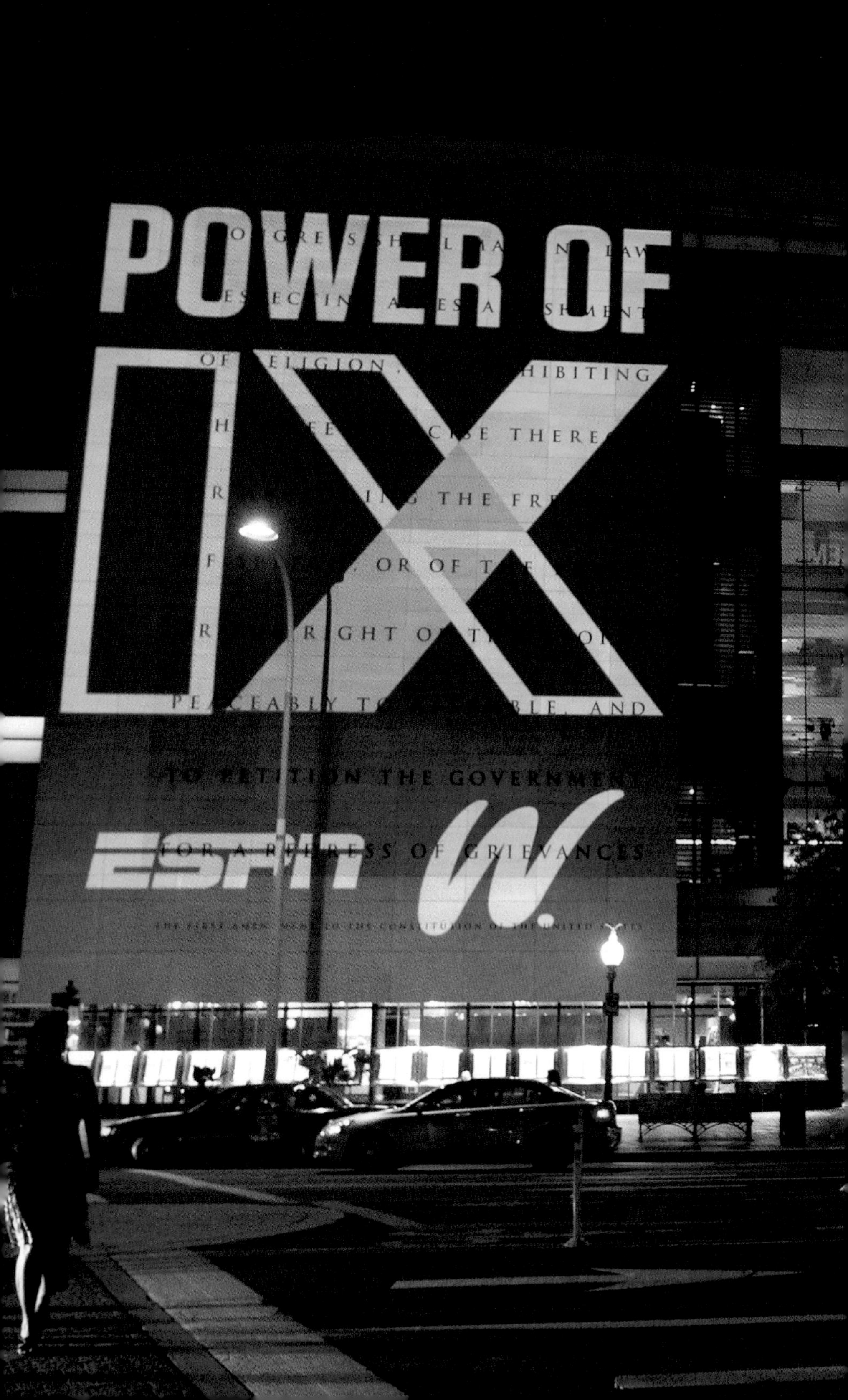
POWER OF
IX
ESPN
W.

The numbers are clear when it comes to women of color
and athletics. Their participation lags behind their
white peers. Girls who do not participate in sports miss out
on the many benefits, from physical fitness to better grades.
To close this gap, school districts and youth sports leaders
have been attempting to understand what would motivate
females of color to take part in an athletic activity. This can
take many forms. It may mean eliminating existing barriers,
such as providing transportation to practices. Or it may
mean introducing girls to sports they know little about.

Another method is to survey girls of color to find
out what athletic activities interest them most. In 2016,
68 percent of female athletes of color played basketball
or track and field.[1] A much wider array of sports exists,
but opportunities to play them vary wildly. By surveying
young female athletes, school districts can create programs
to better serve them. If girls at one school have an
overwhelming interest in golf, for example, investing in
a coach, equipment, and training could go a long way to
increasing participation.

The New York City Department of Education took this
idea to a new level in 2009. That year, the district introduced
double Dutch as a varsity sport in nearly a dozen schools.

Girls in Brooklyn, New York, hone their double Dutch skills.

Most of those schools were in historically African American
neighborhoods, such as Bedford-Stuyvesant and Harlem.
Shani Newsome, a gym teacher in Bedford-Stuyvesant,
explained the importance of double Dutch to girls in the
community. "In Bed-Stuy it's an unspoken rule that you have
to learn how to jump rope," she said. "You can't stay outside
if you don't know how to Double Dutch."[2]

OLD SPORT, NEW COMPETITION

Double Dutch is a rope-skipping game in which two ropes are turned at once in a rope-over-rope motion. Dutch colonists brought the game to New York City during colonial times, and it became a popular pastime for the city's children. Double Dutch requires quick feet, strong hand-eye coordination, and a good sense of timing. Often children sing rhymes or songs as they jump to keep in time with the rhythm of the ropes.

Double Dutch became especially popular among African American girls. Girls added their own style and flair to the sport, and it became an important part of childhood for generations of girls of color. In 2017, a double Dutch tournament held in New York City renewed interest in the sport. "I hope people really start thinking of the contributions of women of color, especially black American women, who elevated the sport and took it to the next level," said Kaisha Johnson, one of the tournament's organizers.[4]

School leaders worked with the National Double Dutch League to create rules and a scoring system. A typical team consists of two people who turn the jump ropes and one or two jumpers. Teams score points for speed and also execution of acrobatic skills, such as cartwheels. Girls have met this new opportunity with enthusiasm. Eighth grader Stephanie Moronta was eager to put her double Dutch skills to the test as she tried out for a spot on a varsity team. "I know a lot of people who like to double-dutch and can do it," said Moronta. "It's going to be exciting going up against other schools. I'm a competitive person, and I really hate to lose."[3]

COMMUNITY SUPPORT

Across the country, community groups are also stepping in to make sure girls of color are not forgotten in the world of sports. In 2004, for example, youth sports leaders created the Boston Girls' Sports and Physical Activities Project. They visited schools and exposed girls to sports they may not have known much about, such as lacrosse. They created programs that catered more to girls' interests, such as dance and yoga. And they created ways to remove barriers to participation, such as sharing vans among different teams to transport girls to practices and games.

On the other side of the country, community groups are working toward the same goal. In 2005, former US Women's National Team soccer stars Brandi Chastain and Julie Foudy joined with women's sports pioneer Marlene Bjornsrud to create the Bay Area Women's

AGE MATTERS

The earlier a child begins sports, the longer she is likely to continue in athletics. Girls of all races begin playing sports later than boys. Forty-seven percent of girls were involved in sports by the age of six. In contrast, 60 percent of six-year-old boys played sports.[5] The disparities grow larger when race and income are added to the mix, with wealthy white children playing sports at the earliest ages. Where a child lives also affects her likelihood to play sports. Suburban children had higher participation rates at earlier ages than their peers in rural and urban settings. Targeting sports programs for girls of color from urban areas at an early age could raise participation rates later in life.

Sports Initiative (BAWSI). It's a free after-school program aimed at girls in second through fifth grade. It is offered to schools that have a large population of students who come from low-income families. This demographic is largely underserved by sports clubs. The program's aim is to expose girls to sports, increase positive feelings toward physical activity, and foster friendships.

Since the program began, its 3,000 female volunteers have served more than 18,000 children. Its resources are changing the lives of girls in positive ways. "My brother gets to go to the gym because my parents pay for it," said one female participant. "But they don't have the money to send me to the gym, so BAWSI is what I get to do for exercise." Another girl explained how the program has changed her daily life: "Before BAWSI, I sat on benches at recess but now I play fun games on the playground."[6]

ELECTED OFFICIALS

Another way communities can improve sports for girls of color is by engaging with leaders in local government. They can ask elected officials to seek funds from federal programs to improve local sports facilities, parks, and playground equipment. For example, the federal government provides money for this type of improvement through the Community Development Block Grant. This money is earmarked for low- and moderate-income areas that could benefit from additional assistance.

Local governments can also help by monitoring school districts to make sure they comply with Title IX. If a school appears out of compliance, the community leaders or elected officials can issue a challenge. When this happens, employees from the Office for Civil Rights travel to the school to investigate the case. If sufficient evidence is found that the school is violating Title IX, investigators issue two documents to school leaders. The first explains the complaint and the findings of the investigation. The second is a plan for how the school can come back into compliance with Title IX.

OUT OF COMPLIANCE

In 2017, students at Red Bluff High School in California filed a lawsuit against the school board, asserting that the school was violating Title IX. The settlement required the school to improve athletic facilities, locker rooms, and sports equipment for female teams. "One thing I learned while working on this case is that almost all high schools are out of compliance with Title IX, not providing girls with equal participation and benefits," said Jane Brunner, one of the lawyers involved in the case. "Hopefully other school districts will wake up and provide girls with equal opportunities in sports without a lawsuit being filed."[7]

PUSHING FURTHER

The future of sports for women of color also largely hinges on leadership, especially in coaching. In 2017, more than 60 percent of women's athletic teams at NCAA schools were

Coquese Washington became the head women's basketball coach at Penn State in 2007.

coached by men, most of whom were white.[8] And when it comes to college athletic directors—the people who hire coaches—the numbers are even worse. In the 2016–17 school year, only four African American women and three Hispanic women worked as Division I athletic directors. Combined, these women made up less than 3 percent of athletic directors at all Division I schools.[9]

"We want the best coaches for our student-athletes," said Penn State women's basketball coach Coquese Washington. "We want the best coaches for our profession. In order for the profession to grow, we want as much diversity as we can have that can accomplish those two things." Washington, who is one of only two African American female head coaches in the Big Ten, believes future improvements begin by making changes at the top level. "If there's greater diversity in athletic administration, I think you see that reflected in hiring practices across all sports."[10]

MEDIA EXPOSURE

According to many experts, one way to increase the number of female athletes of color in the future is to make role models more visible. Making women's sports more available in all forms of media—from television to social networking sites—can go a long way toward this goal.

While traditional media outlets such as network television and local newspapers are slow to change, women's sports have found a number of other media outlets in recent years. In 2010, ESPN launched a website dedicated to female sports called espnW. Its content covers scores, videos, profiles, and news tailored to women's sports fans. The annual espnW: Women + Sports Summit brings together leaders in women's sports in an effort to create more opportunities for females to play sports.

Other forms of media are also highlighting the idea that women have an equal place as athletes. In 2014, the feminine-hygiene brand Always began a new ad campaign: Like a Girl. The ads featured boys and girls of a variety of ethnicities acting out what it meant to throw, run, or fight like a girl. Most boys pretended to drop a ball, run with poor

espnW was founded in 2010 to give more attention to women's sports and women's voices.

The idea of "fighting like a girl" is being turned on its head by modern girls and women.

form, or punch weakly. The girls, however, approached the activities with aggression, determination, and strength.

When the ad ran during the Super Bowl in 2015, more than 115 million people saw it. The response was enormous. Not long after the ad aired, #LikeAGirl became a trending topic on Twitter as women and girls tweeted messages and photos of their athletic triumphs. Shortly after the celebration of females in sports, some men began to criticize the ad. They argued that a 60-second ad that encourages girls to play sports was sexist. This reaction demonstrated once again how far women still have to go before they are on equal footing in sports.

Fortunately, this generation of female athletes has powerful role models to encourage them. In 2016, tennis legend Serena Williams expressed her support in an open letter. In it, she reminded women not to be defined by their skin color or gender but to instead be defined by their potential. "Too often women are not supported enough or are discouraged from choosing their path. I hope together we can change that," wrote Williams. "For me, it was a question of resilience. What others marked as flaws or disadvantages about myself—my race, my gender—I embraced as fuel for my success. I never let anything or anyone define me or my potential. I controlled my future."[12]

DISCUSSION STARTERS

- If you were in charge of a school's athletic programs, what would you do to encourage more girls of color to participate?
- What do you think holds girls of color back from participating in sports?
- Do you think schools should be held accountable for being in compliance with Title IX? Why or why not?

ESSENTIAL FACTS

SIGNIFICANT EVENTS

o In 1964, President Lyndon Johnson signs the Civil Rights Act, which bans discrimination based on race, color, religion, sex, or national origin.

o President Richard Nixon signs Title IX into law in 1972, ensuring that all schools receiving federal funding provide equal opportunities for girls.

o All schools receiving federal funding must comply with Title IX on July 21, 1978.

o In 1996, the Women's National Basketball Association is established, and games begin the next year.

o Radio host Don Imus draws attention to female athletes of color after his 2007 racist comments about the Rutgers women's basketball team.

o The 2012 Olympics in London, England, are the first games in history in which every country participating sends female athletes.

o The Like a Girl ad campaign airs during the 2015 Super Bowl, promoting females in athletics.

KEY PLAYERS

o Althea Gibson broke the color barrier in tennis in 1950, opening the door for other female athletes of color.

o Serena Williams is the world's highest-paid women's tennis player and the winner of more Grand Slam titles than any other man or woman.

o Gabby Douglas is the first gymnast to win gold medals in both the team and individual events in the Olympics, in 2012, as well as the first African American woman to win the individual all-around title.

o Jessica Mendoza is the first woman to be a permanent part of ESPN's top Major League Baseball announcing team.

o Simone Manuel is the first African American woman to win an individual gold medal in swimming.

IMPACT ON SOCIETY

o Women have gained more equality in academics and sports in the 40 years since Title IX passed.

o Many of the opportunities created by Title IX have benefited white women more than women of color.

o Girls who participate in sports have higher grades, have better mental and physical health, and are more likely to have well-paying jobs as adults compared to those who don't participate in sports.

QUOTE

"It is very interesting to see black women going into areas where you really don't see black women competing, with all different body shapes, complexion, and hairstyles being represented. Black women see and feel that there is no door closed to us . . . and that we're not just walking through those doors, but we're dominating."

—*Kaye Wise Whitehead, professor of race and gender studies, Loyola University*

GLOSSARY

administrator
A person who is in a position
of power within a business or
other group.

amateur
A person who competes in a sport
without payment.

circuit
A sports tour that includes a series
of tournaments.

compliance
The state of obeying a law.

deport
To force someone to leave
a country.

discrimination
Unfair treatment of other people,
usually because of race, age,
or gender.

disparity
A great difference between two or
more things.

elite
Superior in some way.

inaugural
The beginning or first part.

integrate
To make schools, parks, and other
facilities available to people of all
races on an equal basis.

physique
The size and structure of a person's body.

poignant
Creating strong feelings.

prestigious
Inspiring respect and admiration; having high status.

quota
A fixed quantity of people, money, or things.

racism
Poor treatment of or violence against people because of their race.

resilience
The ability to recover from difficulties quickly.

revenue
Income, especially of a company or organization and of a substantial nature.

sandlot
An open piece of land children use for playing games.

segregation
The practice of separating groups of people based on race, gender, ethnicity, or other factors.

sexism
Discrimination or prejudice toward people based on their sex.

ADDITIONAL RESOURCES

SELECTED BIBLIOGRAPHY

"Finishing Last: Girls of Color and School Sports Opportunities." National Women's Law Center, 20 Apr. 2015. nwlc.org.

Staurowsky, Ellen J., ed. *Women and Sport: Continuing a Journey of Liberation and Celebration*. Human Kinetics, 2016.

Woolum, Janet. *Outstanding Women Athletes: Who They Are and How They Influenced Sports in America*. Oryx, 1998.

FURTHER READINGS

Harris, Duchess, and Laura K. Murray. *Class and Race*. Abdo, 2019.

Stout, Glenn. *Yes, She Can! Women's Sports Pioneers*. Houghton Mifflin Harcourt, 2011.

Zuckerman, Gregory. *Rising Above: Inspiring Women in Sports*. Philomel Books, 2018.

ONLINE RESOURCES

Booklinks
NONFICTION NETWORK
FREE! ONLINE NONFICTION RESOURCES

To learn more about race and gender in sports, visit **abdobooklinks.com**. These links are routinely monitored and updated to provide the most current information available.

MORE INFORMATION

For more information on this subject, contact or visit the following organizations:

BLACK WOMEN IN SPORT FOUNDATION

4300 Monument Road
Philadelphia, PA 19131
215-877-1925
blackwomeninsport.org

Founded in 1992, the Black Women in Sport Foundation works to increase participation of girls and women of color in sports. It provides community education, instruction, and equipment for girls in a variety of sports, including fencing, lacrosse, and golf.

FAIR PLAY FOR GIRLS IN SPORTS (LEGAL AID AT WORK)

180 Montgomery Street, Suite 600
San Francisco, CA 94104
415-864-8848
legalaidatwork.org

Fair Play for Girls in Sports is run by Legal Aid, an organization that provides free legal services to low-income families. The organization's goal is to ensure all girls receive equal treatment in sports, and it has a special focus on getting girls of color active in sports.

SOURCE NOTES

CHAPTER 1. BARRIER BREAKER

1. "Tennis Great Althea Gibson," *Universal-International News*, July 1957. *YouTube*, 5 June 2012. youtube.com. Accessed 16 Aug. 2018.

2. Althea Gibson. *I Always Wanted to Be Somebody*. Harper & Brothers, 1958. 140.

3. Gibson, *I Always Wanted to Be Somebody*., 140.

4. Gibson, *I Always Wanted to Be Somebody*., 140.

5. Kevin Skiver. "USTA to Honor Althea Gibson, the First Black Grand Slam Champion, with Statue." *CBS Sports*, 1 Mar. 2018. cbssports.com. Accessed 15 Aug. 2018.

CHAPTER 2. LAWS CREATE OPPORTUNITIES

1. "Mamie 'Peanut' Johnson: Oral History." *National Visionary Leadership Project*, n.d. visionaryproject.org. Accessed 16 Aug. 2018.

2. "Mamie 'Peanut' Johnson: Oral History."

3. Brigit Katz. "Remembering Mamie 'Peanut' Johnson, the First Woman to Take the Mound as a Major-League Pitcher." *Smithsonian*, 26 Dec. 2007. smithsonian.com. Accessed 15 Aug. 2018.

4. Biography.com editors. "Toni Stone Biography." *Biography.com*, 4 Feb. 2016. biography.com. Accessed 15 Aug. 2018.

5. "Title IX of the Education Amendments of 1972." *US Department of Justice*, n.d. justice.gov. Accessed 15 Aug. 2018.

6. "Women in America: Indicators of Social and Economic Well-Being." *White House Council on Women and Girls*, Mar. 2011. digitalcommons.ilr.cornell.edu. Accessed 16 Aug. 2018. 17, 21–22.

CHAPTER 3. BARRIERS

1. "Go Out and Play: Youth Sports in America." *Women's Sports Foundation*, Oct. 2008. womenssportsfoundation.org. Accessed 16 Aug. 2018. 2, 15.

2. "About Us." *Boston Showstoppers*, n.d. bostonshowstoppers.com. Accessed 16 Aug. 2018.

3. William C. Rhoden. "Black and White Women Far from Equal Under Title IX." *New York Times*, 10 June 2012. nytimes.com. Accessed 15 Aug. 2018.

4. "Finishing Last: Girls of Color and School Sports Opportunities." *National Women's Law Center*, 20 Apr. 2015. nwlc.org. Accessed 16 Aug. 2018. 7.

5. Robert García et al. "Economic Stimulus, Green Space, and Equal Justice." *The City Project*, Apr. 2009. cityprojectca.org. Accessed 16 Aug. 2018. 8–9.

6. Robert García. "Bringing the San Gabriel Mountains Closer to the People." *The City Project*, 9 Feb. 2012. cityprojectca.org. Accessed 16 Aug. 2018.

7. Candace Buckner. "Hispanic Girls Face Many Obstacles to Playing Sports." *Kansas City Star*, 9 July 2009, hispanic-marketing.com. Accessed 15 Aug. 2018.

8. "Pay-to-Play Sports Keeping Lower-Income Kids Out of the Game." *University of Michigan*, C. S. Mott Children's Hospital, 14 May 2012. mottpoll.org. Accessed 15 Aug. 2018.

9. Les Carpenter. "'It's Only Working for the White Kids': American Soccer's Diversity Problem." *Guardian*, 1 June 2016. theguardian.com. Accessed 15 Aug. 2018.

CHAPTER 4. YOUTH AND COLLEGE SPORTS

1. "Finishing Last: Girls of Color and School Sports Opportunities." *National Women's Law Center*, 20 Apr. 2015. nwlc.org. Accessed 16 Aug. 2018. 6.

2. Teresa Wiltz. "Racial and Ethnic Disparities Persist in Teen Pregnancy Rates." *Pew Charitable Trusts*, 3 Mar. 2015. pewtrusts.org. Accessed 15 Aug. 2018.

3. "Finishing Last: Girls of Color and School Sports Opportunities," 7.

4. Christina M. Tapper. "SportsKid of the Year 2014: Mo'ne Davis." *Sports Illustrated Kids*, 1 Dec. 2014. sikids.com. Accessed 15 Aug. 2018.

5. "Finishing Last: Girls of Color and School Sports Opportunities," 7.

6. "Finishing Last: Girls of Color and School Sports Opportunities," 1–5.

7. "Finishing Last: Girls of Color and School Sports Opportunities," 3.

8. "Finishing Last: Girls of Color and School Sports Opportunities," 4.

9. Alia Wong. "Where Girls Are Missing Out on High-School Sports." *Atlantic*, 26 June 2015. theatlantic.com. Accessed 15 Aug. 2018.

10. Richard Lapchick. "College Sport Racial and Gender Report Card." *The Institute for Diversity and Ethics in Sports*, 2017. tidesport.org. Accessed 16 Aug. 2018. 20.

11. Lapchick, "College Sports Racial and Gender Report Card," 5.

12. Lapchick, "College Sports Racial and Gender Report Card," 20.

13. William C. Rhoden. "Black and White Women Far from Equal Under Title IX." *New York Times*, 10 June 2012. nytimes.com. Accessed 15 Aug. 2018.

14. Shannon Ryan. "College Sports Needs More Women—and Women of Color—in Coaching Ranks." *Chicago Tribune*, 17 Apr. 2017. chicagotribune.com. Accessed 15 Aug. 2018.

15. "Perceived Barriers for Ethnic Minority Females in Collegiate Athletics Careers." *NCAA*, Feb. 2016. ncaa.org. Accessed 16 Aug. 2018. 1–2.

CHAPTER 5. OLYMPIANS

1. David Climber. "Olympics Great Stage for Women." *Tennessean*, 5 Aug. 1996. newspapers.com. 18.

2. Rima Maktabi and Jon Jensen. "Qatar's First Female Olympians on Target to Make History." *CNN*, 7 May 2012. cnn.com. Accessed 15 Aug. 2018.

3. Lautaro Grinspan. "Why the Diversity of Team USA Matters." *USA Today College*, 19 Aug. 2016. college.usatoday.com. Accessed 15 Aug. 2018.

4. "2016 U.S. Olympic Team." *Team USA*, n.d., teamusa.org. Accessed 15 Aug. 2018.

5. Rick Maese. "Trying to Make Team USA Look More Like America." *Washington Post*, 2 Feb. 2018. washingtonpost.com. Accessed 15 Aug. 2018.

6. "#Blackgirlmagic: African-American Women Take Spotlight at Rio Olympics." *NBC News*, 20 Aug. 2016. nbcnews.com. Accessed 15 Aug. 2018.

7. "USA Swimming Foundation Announces 5–10 Percent Increase in Swimming Ability among U.S. Children." *USA Swimming Foundation*, 13 July 2017. usaswimmingfoundation.org. Accessed 15 Aug. 2018.

8. Simone Manuel. "Simone Manuel: We Need to Get Rid of the Racial Stereotypes That Surround Swimming." *Essence*, 23 Aug. 2017. essence.com. Accessed 15 Aug. 2018.

9. Gretchen Reynolds. "Will Simone Manuel Inspire More Black Children to Swim?" *New York Times*, 16 Aug. 2016. nytimes.com. Accessed 22 Aug. 2018.

10. "#Blackgirlmagic: African-American Women Take Spotlight at Rio Olympics."

11. Karen Rosen. "Ibtihaj Muhammad Officially Becomes First Team USA Athlete to Compete in Hijab at Olympics." *Team USA*, 8 Aug. 2016. teamusa.org. Accessed 15 Aug. 2018.

13. "Excellence Takes Time." *Sport for Life*, n.d. sportforlife.ca. Accessed 15 Aug. 2018.

14. Jennifer Calfas. "'It's About Making History.' These Athletes Are Breaking Barriers at the 2018 Winter Olympics." *Time*, 8 Feb. 2018. time.com. Accessed 15 Aug. 2018.

CHAPTER 6. THE PROS

1. "History of the WNBA." *WNBA*, 3 May 2002. wnba.com. Accessed 15 Aug. 2018.

2. Richard Lapchick. "The 2017 WNBA Racial and Gender Report Card." *The Institute for Diversity and Ethics in Sport*, 15 Nov. 2017. tidesport.org. Accessed 16 Aug. 2018. 1.

3. "WNBA Scores High on Racial and Gender Report Card." *ESPN*, 2 Nov. 2016. espn.com. Accessed 15 Aug. 2018.

4. Jason Belzer. "The Most Powerful Women in US Sports 2018." *Forbes*, 27 Mar. 2018. forbes.com. Accessed 15 Aug. 2018.

5. "Stephen Curry NBA Salary." *HoopsHype*, n.d. hoopshype.com. Accessed 15 Aug. 2018.

6. Jessica Dickler. "This WNBA Superstar Earns Just 20% of an NBA Player's Salary." *CNBC*, 3 Oct. 2017. cnbc.com. Accessed 15 Aug. 2018.

7. Richard Lapchick. "The WNBA Leads All Sports Leagues in Diversity and Inclusion." *ESPN*, 16 Nov. 2017. espn.com. Accessed 15 Aug. 2018.

8. Dickler, "This WNBA Superstar Earns Just 20% of an NBA Player's Salary."

9. Stephanie Yang. "When It Comes to Diversity, Is Women's Soccer Making Progress?" *Vice Sports*, 27 Feb. 2017. vicesports.com. Accessed 15 Aug. 2018.

10. Yang, "When It Comes to Diversity, Is Women's Soccer Making Progress?"

11. Yang, "When It Comes to Diversity, Is Women's Soccer Making Progress?"

12. "Market Watch: NWSL Salary Cap." *Soccer America*, 15 Mar. 2018. socceramerica.com. Accessed 15 Aug. 2018.

13. "MLS Players Union Announces That It Has Ratified Collective Bargaining Agreement." *MLS Soccer*, 16 July 2015. mlssoccer.com. Accessed 15 Aug. 2018.

14. Maggie Mertens. "Women's Soccer Is a Feminist Issue." *Atlantic*, 5 June 2015. theatlantic.com. Accessed 15 Aug. 2018.

15. Kurt Badenhausen. "Serena Williams Heads the Highest-Paid Female Athletes 2017." *Forbes*, 14 Aug. 2017. forbes.com. Accessed 15 Aug. 2018.

16. Chris Chase. "Serena Williams Ends Indian Wells Boycott, 14 Years after Racist Incident." *USA Today*, 4 Feb. 2015. ftw.usatoday.com. Accessed 15 Aug. 2018.

17. Nathan Hurst. "Media Microaggressions against Female Olympic Athletes Up 40 Percent." *University of Missouri*, 13 June 2017. nbsubscribe.missouri.edu. Accessed 15 Aug. 2018.

18. Hurst, "Media Microaggressions against Female Olympic Athletes Up 40 Percent."

19. Mechelle Voepel. "LPGA History Is Upon Us: Sadena Parks and Cheyenne Woods Have Arrived." *espnW*, 18 Feb. 2015. espn.com. Accessed 15 Aug. 2018.

20. Anya Alvarez. "The New Face of Golf: The LPGA Is More Diverse Than Ever, but Is That Enough to Grow the Game?" *Excelle Sports*, 20 Jan. 2017. excellesports.com. Accessed 15 Aug. 2018.

21. Alvarez, "The New Face of Golf."

CHAPTER 7. THE MEDIA

1. @MarkMravic. "And here some people (ahem, @Andy_Benoit) argue that women's soccer isn't worth watching." *Twitter*, 22 June 2015, 3:36 p.m. twitter.com. Accessed 16 Aug. 2018.

2. Jessica Chasmar. "*Sports Illustrated* Writer Says Women's Sports 'Not Worth Watching.'" *Washington Times*, 23 June 2015. washingtontimes.com. Accessed 15 Aug. 2018.

3. Chasmar, "*Sports Illustrated* Writer Says Women's Sports 'Not Worth Watching.'"

4. Kelly Carrion. "Baseball Analyst Jessica Mendoza Makes History, Draws Sexist Backlash." *NBC News*, 7 Oct. 2015. nbcnews.com. Accessed 15 Aug. 2018.

5. Sara Morrison. "Media Is 'Failing Women'—Sports Journalism Particularly So." *Poynter*, 19 Feb. 2014. poynter.org. Accessed 15 Aug. 2018.

6. Amanda Ottaway. "Why Don't People Watch Women's Sports?" *Nation*, 20 July 2016. thenation.com. Accessed 15 Aug. 2018.

7. "Media Coverage and Female Athletes." *Twin Cities Public Television*, 1 Dec. 2013. video.tpt.org. Accessed 16 Aug. 2018.

8. Vanessa Williams. "Gabby Douglas's Hair Sets Off Twitter Debate, but Some Ask: 'What's the Fuss?'" *Washington Post*. 3 Aug. 2012. washingtonpost.com. Accessed 15 Aug. 2018.

9. Williams, "Gabby Douglas's Hair Sets Off Twitter Debate."

10. Robin Vealey and Melissa Chase. *Best Practice for Youth Sport*. Human Kinetics, 2016.

11. James Kratch. "Retiring Don Imus Expresses 'Regret' for Rutgers Racial Remark: 'I Knew Better.'" *NJ.com*, 27 Mar. 2018. nj.com. Accessed 15 Aug. 2018.

12. "Media—Images and Words in Women's Sports." *Women's Sports Foundation*, n.d. womenssportsfoundation.org. Accessed 15 Aug. 2018.

CHAPTER 8. THE FUTURE

1. "Race and Sport." *Women's Sports Foundation*, n.d., womenssportsfoundation.org. Accessed 15 Aug. 2018.

2. Winnie Hu. "Double Dutch Gets Status in the Schools." *New York Times*, 31 July 2008. nytimes.com. Accessed 15 Aug. 2018.

3. Hu, "Double Dutch Gets Status in the Schools."

4. Erica Euse. "Double Dutch Is Back and It Is Breathtaking." *Vice*, 4 Aug. 2017. vice.com. Accessed 15 Aug. 2018.

5. "Go Out and Play: Youth Sports in America." *Women's Sports Foundation*, Oct. 2008. womenssportsfoundation.org. Accessed 16 Aug. 2018. 119–140.

6. "About BAWSI." *Bay Area Women's Sports Initiative*, n.d. bawsi.org. Accessed 15 Aug. 2018.

7. "Northern California High School Moves toward Equality with Title IX Settlement." *Legal Aid at Work*, 15 Nov. 2017. legalaidatwork.org. Accessed 15 Aug. 2018.

8. Shannon Ryan. "College Sports Needs More Women—and Women of Color—in Coaching Ranks." *Chicago Tribune*, 17 Apr. 2017. chicagotribune.com. Accessed 15 Aug. 2018.

9. Richard Lapchick. "College Sport Racial and Gender Report Card." *The Institute for Diversity and Ethics in Sports*, 2017. tidesport.org. Accessed 16 Aug. 2018.

10. Ryan, "College Sports Needs More Women—and Women of Color—in Coaching Ranks."

11. Katie Thomas. "ESPN Slowly Introducing Online Brand for Women." *New York Times*, 15 Oct. 2010. nytimes.com. Accessed 22 Aug. 2018.

12. Megan Lasher. "Serena Williams Wrote a Letter to Every Single Woman in the World." *Time*, 30 Nov. 2016. time.com. Accessed 15 Aug. 2018.

INDEX

ABOUT THE AUTHORS

DUCHESS HARRIS, JD, PHD

Professor Harris is the chair of the American Studies department at Macalester College and curator of the Duchess Harris Collection of ABDO books. She is the author and coauthor of recently released ABDO books including *Hidden Human Computers: The Black Women of NASA*, *Black Lives Matter*, and *Race and Policing*.

Before working with ABDO, she authored several other books on the topics of race, culture, and American history. She served as an associate editor for *Litigation News*, the American Bar Association Section of Litigation's quarterly flagship publication, and was the first editor in chief of *Law Raza*, an interactive online journal covering race and the law, published at William Mitchell College of Law. She has earned a PhD in American Studies from the University of Minnesota and a JD from William Mitchell College of Law.

KATE CONLEY

Kate Conley has been writing nonfiction books for children for more than a decade. When she's not writing, Conley spends her time reading, drawing, and solving crossword puzzles. She lives in Minnesota with her husband and two children.